I0418412

CONTENTS

DISCLAIMER: I am not a doctor or a medical professional, and therefore, this book is not intended to prescribe long or short water fasts. Pregnant women, nursing mothers, children, and those on heavy medication should abstain from any food fasting. If you're on medication or have a condition that might hinder you from fasting, consult your doctor before starting.

VLADIMIR SAVCHUK

21 DAYS OF PRAYER AND FASTING

A DEVOTIONAL GUIDE

ISBN: 979-8-89314-065-1 paperback

WEEK 1: BUILDING AN ALTAR
[Days 1 to 7]

The first week of this fast is about turning your attention fully to God and preparing the altar of your heart. You are not just skipping meals. You are shifting your appetite and saying, "Lord, You are my food." As your body feels hunger, your spirit is learning to feast on His presence and His Word in a fresh way.

These early days expose how attached we are to comfort, routine, and distraction. God uses this to lovingly search the hidden places of the heart. He begins to deal with motives, secret attitudes, and the quiet compromises that have dulled your fire. This is not to condemn you, but to cleanse and realign you.

In Week 1, expect God to deepen your hunger, purify your desires, and rekindle the flame on the altar of your heart. You are setting the tone for the rest of the fast. As you humble yourself, repent, and give Him your full attention, the foundation is laid for deeper freedom and greater encounters in the weeks ahead.

DAY 1: Fasting Is Feasting on God

Key Scripture:

"But seek first the kingdom of God and His righteousness, and all these things shall be added to you." Matthew 6:33

Supporting Scriptures:

Psalm 63:1 | Luke 12:31
Fasting is not about what you are losing. It is about whom you are gaining. When you say no to the plate, you are saying yes to a deeper awareness of God's presence. Your body may feel empty, but your spirit is being invited to feast on the One who truly satisfies. Jesus said His food was to do the will of the Father. That same grace is available to you in this fast.

The first day often exposes how much comfort we draw from routines, snacks, and little distractions. Each time you feel that pull, do not just endure it. Redirect it. Let hunger become a signal that turns your heart toward Jesus. You are not starving; you are shifting your appetite. You are training your soul to understand that life does not flow from bread alone, but from every word that proceeds from God.

Today, lift your expectations. The God who invited you into this fast is the same God who will sustain you through it. He is not watching you struggle. He is drawing near to you. As you lay aside food, you are making room in your schedule, in your emotions, and in your attention for Him. This is where the real feast begins.

Practical Steps:

1. Set a clear focus for this fast. Write one main area where you want to see God move.

2. Replace at least one meal time with worship and reading Psalm 63.

3. When hunger hits, whisper: "Jesus, You are my food. I feast on Your presence."

Prayer Points:

1. Lord, make my hunger for You greater than my hunger for food.

2. Father, purify my motives for fasting.

3. Jesus, become my satisfaction and delight.

4. Holy Spirit, strengthen my body and calm my mind.

5. God, let this fast awaken my first love for You again.

_____

_____

_____

_____

_____

_____

_____

DAY 2: Training the Heart to Seek God

Key Scripture:

"Watch and pray, lest you enter into temptation. The spirit indeed is willing, but the flesh is weak." Matthew 26:41

Supporting Scriptures:

Galatians 5:16 | Romans 8:5

Fasting slows the noise long enough for you to see what usually hides under the surface. On this second day, the body often complains, and the mind may feel foggy. Do not despise this moment. The discomfort is not a punishment. It is a mirror. It shows you where your strength ends and where God's strength begins.

When you choose prayer instead of frustration, you are training your heart to seek God, not comfort. The flesh wants relief, but the Spirit is inviting you into deeper dependence. Each time hunger rises, let it become a call to watch and pray. This is not a casual devotion. This is training. You are learning to walk by the Spirit and not be ruled by cravings, moods, or impulses.

The Lord is using these hours to tune your inner life. As you yield, He starts exposing attitudes, fears, and hidden attachments. Do not run from that exposure. Invite Him into it. Today, ask the Holy Spirit to rewire your desires so that seeking God becomes your first response, not your last resort.

Practical Steps:

1. Sit in silence for five minutes before you pray and simply say, "Holy Spirit, here I am."

2. Notice one area where your flesh resisted today and deliberately surrender it to God in prayer.

3. Repeat Galatians 5:16 every time you feel hunger or irritation rise.

_____

_____

_____

_____

_____

_____

_____

_____

Prayer Points:

1. Lord, strengthen my inner life to seek You first.

2. Help me walk by the Spirit, not by my emotions.

3. Expose and heal any hidden resistance in my heart.

4. Give me grace to endure this fast with joy, not complaining.

5. Draw my attention back to You throughout the day, even in small moments.

_____

_____

_____

_____

_____

_____

DAY 3: Breaking the Power of Distraction

Key Scripture:

"My voice You shall hear in the morning, O Lord; in the morning I will direct it to You, and I will look up." Psalm 5:3

Supporting Scriptures:

Proverbs 4:25–27 | Hebrews 12:2
Fasting is not only about food. It is also about focus. Our generation is drowning in distractions. Notifications, constant scrolling, noise in the mind. During a fast, God invites you to confront the subtle idols of distraction that steal your attention and drain your spiritual strength. The battle for your destiny is often a battle for your focus.

When you rise to seek God, you are not doing a religious routine. You are taking your place as a commander of the day. Fasting helps you reclaim those first moments, redirecting them from the phone to the throne, from worry to worship.

Today, ask the Lord to break the hold of distraction over your life. As your body abstains from food, let your heart abstain from noise. Turn your gaze to Jesus. He is the Author and Finisher of your faith. As you look to Him, the clutter will begin to lose its power.

Practical Steps:

1. Begin your day with scripture and prayer before you touch your phone.

2. Choose one distraction you will fast from today in addition to food.

3. Take a short walk or pause in silence and simply repeat, "Jesus, my eyes are on You."

_____

_____

_____

_____

_____

_____

_____

_____

_____

Prayer Points:

1. Lord, free me from every subtle distraction that dulls my hunger for You.

2. Teach me to command my mornings with prayer and the Word.

3. Fix my eyes on Jesus in the middle of busyness and pressure.

4. Heal my mind from constant noise and restlessness.

5. Let my attention become an offering that honors You.

_____

_____

_____

_____

_____

_____

DAY 4: Holiness in the Hidden Places

Key Scripture:

"Search me, O God, and know my heart; try me, and know my anxieties." Psalm 139:23

Supporting Scriptures:

1 Peter 1:15 | Isaiah 58

Fasting exposes more than hunger. It exposes the heart. When you quiet your flesh, things that were buried under busyness begin to surface. God does not reveal this to shame you. He reveals it to heal you. True fasting is more than skipping meals. It is allowing the Lord to confront motives, attitudes, and compromises that no one else sees.

Holiness begins in the hidden places. It is easy to appear spiritual while the heart still clings to offense, secret sin, or pride. In this fast, the Holy Spirit is gently knocking on doors you have kept closed. He may bring up conversations, memories, or areas of obedience you have delayed. Do not push them away. Invite His light into them.

Isaiah 58 shows that God is not impressed by outward fasting while injustice and strife remain. He wants transformation, not performance. Today, let your fast become an altar where you lay down what He is highlighting. When you surrender the hidden places, you make room for His presence to dwell in greater measure.

Practical Steps:

1. Ask the Holy Spirit, "Is there anything in me that grieves You?" Write down what He shows.

2. Confess any sin, compromise, or unforgiveness He exposes, and receive His cleansing.

3. Read Isaiah 58 and turn it into a personal prayer.

_____

_____

_____

_____

_____

_____

_____

_____

Prayer Points:

1. Lord, shine Your light into the hidden places of my heart.

2. Cleanse me from secret faults and wrong motives.

3. Give me grace to walk in holiness, not just outward discipline.

4. Break every habit that keeps me distant from Your presence.

5. Let this fast become a turning point in my character.

DAY 5: Fire on the Altar of Your Heart

Key Scripture:

"For our God is a consuming fire."
Hebrews 12:29

Supporting Scriptures:

Psalm 119:40 | Luke 24:32

In Scripture, fire represents the presence of God, His purity, and His power. On the altar of the Old Testament, fire was never meant to go out. In the New Covenant, your heart is that altar. Fasting makes room for fresh fire. It positions you where the Holy Spirit can burn away what does not belong and ignite what has grown cold.

Many believers love God, yet their prayer life is faint, their worship is dry, and their passion is low. The issue is not that God has changed. The fire has simply been buried under the ashes of distraction, disappointment, and compromise. When you fast, you are clearing the altar. You are saying, "Lord, breathe on these coals again."

Ask the Lord today for fresh fire. Not emotional hype, but holy intensity. A burning love for Jesus that cannot be silenced. A desire for His presence that is stronger than your desire for comfort. God's fire refines, but it also empowers. It will burn away apathy and ignite courage, boldness, and obedience.

Practical Steps:

1. Take time to worship without asking for anything. Focus only on who God is.

2. Pray in the Spirit, or pray out loud, longer than you normally would. Stretch your desire.

3. Ask God specifically to reignite any area where you have grown spiritually cold.

_____

_____

_____

_____

_____

_____

_____

Prayer Points:

1. Lord, let Your consuming fire fall on the altar of my heart.

2. Burn away apathy, compromise, and spiritual laziness.

3. Ignite fresh passion for prayer, worship, and Your Word.

4. Fill me with boldness to obey what You speak.

5. Let my life become a testimony of Your fire to others.

_____

_____

_____

_____

_____

_____

DAY 6: Breakthrough in Relationships

Key Scripture:

"Above all, love each other deeply, because love covers over a multitude of sins." 1 Peter 4:8

Supporting Scriptures:

Psalm 147:3 | Proverbs 17:9

God cares deeply about the relationships in your life. He is not only interested in your spiritual growth but also in the people He has placed around you. Many believers fast and pray for personal breakthrough but overlook the connections that shape their daily life. Today is a day to bring your relationships before the Lord. Whether it is with parents, siblings, children, friends, mentors, or coworkers, God wants to bring restoration and breakthrough. Healing in relationships starts with humility, prayer, and letting God address what we cannot fix on our own.

Ask the Holy Spirit to reveal the relationships that need His touch. Surrender the emotions and misunderstandings you have been carrying. Lay the disappointments at the feet of Jesus. Ask Him to soften every hardened place in your heart and renew love where it has grown weak. Pray for His wisdom to guide your words and decisions so you do not lean on your own understanding. Remember, you cannot change another person's heart, but you can let God change yours.

As God works in you, He creates room for Him to work in the relationships around you. Today, believe that God can restore what was damaged, strengthen what is weak, and reconcile what has been divided. Nothing is too hard for Him. As you fast, declare that God is bringing breakthrough in every relationship connected to your life.

Practical Steps:

1. Bring each relationship to the Lord and ask Him to step into the places that need His touch.

2. Choose to forgive where it's needed and ask the Holy Spirit to help you let it go from the heart.

3. Take one small, Spirit-led step toward reconciliation as He prompts you.

_____

_____

_____

_____

_____

_____

_____

_____

_____

Prayer Points:

1. Lord, touch every relationship in my life and bring Your healing where it is needed.

2. Holy Spirit, reveal to me where I may have been at fault and show me the steps I need to take toward reconciliation.

3. Soften my heart and fill me with Your love, patience, and understanding.

4. Help me forgive freely and release every hurt into Your hands.

5. Bring restoration, peace, and unity to every connection that has been strained.

_____

_____

_____

_____

DAY 7: Repentance That Brings Revival

Key Scripture:

"If My people who are called by My name will humble themselves, and pray and seek My face, and turn from their wicked ways, then I will hear from heaven, and will forgive their sin and heal their land." 2 Chronicles 7:14

Supporting Scriptures:

Isaiah 58:6–9 | 1 John 1:9

The first week of a fast often brings deep conviction. You have been feeling your weakness, and at the same time, sensing God's nearness. This is mercy. Fasting humbles you. It confronts pride, self-reliance, and hidden sin. But heaven's answer to repentance is always restoration, never condemnation.

Isaiah 58 reveals God's heart. He does not only want a hunger strike. He wants hearts turned, chains broken, yokes lifted, and relationships restored. When you repent, you are not coming to an angry Judge. You are returning to a loving Father who longs to heal you. Repentance is not humiliation. It is alignment.

Today, take time to come clean before God. Let this be a day where you close old doors. Confess what needs to be confessed. Forgive who needs to be forgiven. Release what has kept you stuck. As you turn, God hears. He forgives. He heals. This is how you finish the first week: lighter, cleaner, more aligned with His heart.

Practical Steps:

1. Ask the Holy Spirit to show you specific areas where you need to repent or reconcile.

2. If possible, make a call or send a message to someone you need to forgive or ask forgiveness from.

3. Read Isaiah 58 and underline what God promises to do when His people fast His way.

_____

_____

_____

_____

_____

_____

_____

Prayer Points:

1. Lord, I humble myself before You. Search my heart and cleanse me.

2. I repent for any pride, unbelief, or disobedience in my life.

3. Heal my relationships and give me grace to forgive.

4. Break every yoke and chain that has kept me bound.

5. Let the second week of this fast be marked by freedom and fresh grace.

_____

_____

_____

_____

_____

_____

WEEK 2: BREAKING SPIRITUAL CHAINS

(Days 8 to 14)

The second week moves from inner preparation to spiritual confrontation. By now, your flesh has been weakened and your spirit is more sensitive. God begins to highlight patterns of delay, bondage, and resistance that have followed you and your family for years. He is not only healing you. He is confronting what has tried to hold your destiny.

In this phase, you will pray against delay, stagnation, and evil patterns. You will stand in the gap for your bloodline, renouncing wrong altars and inviting the fire of God to destroy long-standing yokes. You will learn to command your mornings, sanctify your nights, and take your place as a watchman over your home.

Week 2 is where atmospheres begin to shift. Expect God to expose and break chains, to disappoint the plans of the enemy, and to release fresh authority in your prayers. What once intimidated you will begin to lose its grip as you stand in the victory of the cross and enforce what Jesus has already finished.

DAY 8: Confronting the Spirit of Delay

Key Scripture:

"And about the eleventh hour he went out and found others standing idle... He said to them, 'You also go into the vineyard, and whatever is right you will receive.'" Matthew 20:6–7

Supporting Scriptures:

Joel 2:25 | Psalm 40:1

Delay is one of the enemy's cruelest weapons. It is not just about time. It is about hope. When answers seem slow, the heart can begin to believe that nothing will ever change. Fasting brings you face to face with delays in your life and family, not to depress you, but to empower you to confront them in the Spirit.

The God you serve is the God of the eleventh hour. When men say it is late, He calls it His time. He can compress years into days. He can restore wasted seasons with one move of His hand. Through fasting, you are bringing your delays to His altar and declaring that delay is not your destiny.

Today, refuse to accept stagnation as normal. Bring every long-standing issue before the Lord: the unanswered prayers, the closed doors, the repeated cycles. Cry out with faith, not despair. The God of the eleventh hour is able to break the power of delay and release you into His appointed time.

Practical Steps:

1. Make a list of areas where you have experienced long delay and bring them specifically before God.

2. Declare Joel 2:25 out loud over your life and family.

3. Refuse to agree with hopelessness. When it comes, speak out: "My times are in God's hands."

_____

_____

_____

_____

_____

_____

_____

_____

Prayer Points:

1. Lord, confront every spirit of delay operating in my life.

2. Break cycles of stagnation and waiting without reward.

3. Restore the years that were stolen, wasted, or delayed.

4. Release divine appointments and open doors in this season.

5. Let my life become a testimony that You are the God of the eleventh hour.

_____

_____

_____

_____

_____

_____

DAY 9: Divine Compensation

Key Scripture:

"Instead of your shame you shall have double honor, and instead of confusion they shall rejoice in their portion." Isaiah 61:7

Supporting Scriptures:

Joel 2:26–27 | Romans 8:28

God does not only restore what was lost. He compensates. Where the enemy brought shame, God promises double honor. Where there was confusion, He brings clarity and joy. Fasting positions you to receive this divine compensation. You are not begging God to feel sorry for you. You are aligning with what He already desires to do.

Many have walked through seasons of ridicule, failed attempts, and hidden disappointments. Tears were shed in private while a brave face was shown in public. Heaven saw every moment. The same God who collected your tears is now preparing your testimony. He does not ignore pain. He transforms it into promotion.

Today, dare to believe for double. Not out of greed, but out of faith in His nature. Ask Him to turn shame into honor, loss into gain, and delay into acceleration. Your story will not end in embarrassment. It will end in glory that points back to Him.

Practical Steps:

1. Identify one area where you experienced shame or loss, and ask God specifically for double honor there.

2. Meditate on Isaiah 61 and write down promises that speak directly to your situation.

3. Thank God in advance for the compensation you have not yet seen.

_____

_____

_____

_____

_____

_____

_____

Prayer Points:

1. Lord, turn my shame into double honor for Your name.

2. Redeem every painful chapter and use it for Your glory.

3. Replace confusion with clarity and joy in my heart.

4. Let my testimony silence the voice of my accusers.

5. Make my life a sign that You restore and compensate Your children.

DAY 10: Breaking Evil Altars

Key Scripture:

"But this is what you shall do to them: you shall destroy their altars, break their sacred pillars…" Deuteronomy 7:5

Supporting Scriptures:

Judges 6:25–26 | Colossians 2:14–15
Some battles are not random. They are patterns. The same cycles repeat: rising and falling, almost there but never there, open doors that suddenly close. Behind many of these patterns are spiritual altars and agreements made before you were even born. Fasting is a powerful weapon God uses to confront those unseen structures.

In Judges 6, God told Gideon to tear down the altar in his father's house before raising a new one to the Lord. In Christ, the cross has already disarmed principalities and powers. Yet God often leads you to enforce that victory over specific areas of your bloodline. You do not fight for victory. You fight from victory, applying what Jesus finished.

Today, stand in that authority. Renounce every known and unknown covenant that does not belong to God. Declare that your life belongs to Jesus alone. As you fast and pray, you are raising a new altar in your family line, one that speaks of blessing, freedom, and obedience.

Practical Steps:

1. Ask the Holy Spirit to reveal any recurring patterns in your family line. Write them down.

2. Verbally renounce any occult, witchcraft, or idolatrous involvement you know of, covering it with the blood of Jesus.

3. Take communion if possible and declare that the cross is the only altar that speaks over your life.

_____

_____

_____

_____

_____

_____

_____

Prayer Points:

1. Lord, expose and uproot every evil altar speaking against my destiny.

2. Break every generational pattern of failure, delay, and affliction.

3. I renounce every covenant, known or unknown, that is not from You.

4. Let the blood of Jesus silence every accusation over my life and family.

5. Establish a new altar of worship, obedience, and blessing in my bloodline.

_____

_____

_____

_____

_____

_____

DAY II: Crossing Your Red Sea

Key Scripture:

"Do not be afraid. Stand still, and see the salvation of the Lord, which He will accomplish for you today… The Lord will fight for you, and you shall hold your peace." Exodus 14:13–14

Supporting Scriptures:

Exodus 14:21–22 | Psalm 77:14

Every believer faces a Red Sea moment. You see promise ahead, but an impossible barrier stands in front, and pressure pursues from behind. Logic says there is no way. Heaven says, "Lift your rod and move forward." Fasting sharpens your awareness of God's power in those Red Sea places where human effort has failed.

The God of Moses has not changed. He still makes a way where there is no way. He still parts seas, silences Pharaohs, and turns panic into praise. When you fast and pray, you are not ignoring the sea. You are speaking to it with the authority of God's Word and declaring that impossibility is not the final voice.

Today, bring your Red Sea to the Lord. Is it a legal battle, a debt, a medical report, a physical limitation, or a sickness that has challenged your faith? Stand still on the inside as you obey His instructions. The Lord will fight for you. The same waters that blocked you will become the testimony of His deliverance.

Practical Steps:

1. Name your "Red Sea" out loud before God and surrender it fully to Him.

2. Find one scripture that speaks to your situation and declare it repeatedly throughout the day.

3. Choose one small step of obedience that demonstrates you are moving forward in faith.

_____

_____

_____

_____

_____

_____

_____

_____

Prayer Points:

1. Lord, stand between me and every pursuing enemy like a wall of fire.

2. Part every Red Sea that blocks Your will in my life.

3. Turn my fear into faith and my panic into praise.

4. Let those who mocked my faith see Your mighty hand at work.

5. Make this situation a lasting testimony of Your power.

_____

_____

_____

_____

_____

_____

_____

DAY 12: The Anointing That Destroys the Yoke

Key Scripture:

"It shall come to pass in that day that his burden will be taken away from your shoulder, and his yoke from your neck, and the yoke will be destroyed because of the anointing." Isaiah 10:27

Supporting Scriptures:

Hebrews 12:29 | Acts 10:38

There are burdens you can shake off with discipline. There are others that only the anointing can destroy. Fasting invites the fire of God to touch yokes that have sat on your life for years. Bondages of addiction, fear, oppression, and torment bow under the weight of God's presence.

Jesus went about doing good and healing all who were oppressed by the devil because God was with Him. That same presence is at work when you fast and pray. The consuming fire of God does not only make you feel warm. It burns away the chains that held you, often in ways that are deeper than you realize at the moment.

Today, ask the Lord for the kind of breakthrough that cannot be explained by willpower or self-help. Ask Him to destroy the yokes, not just loosen them. As you do, believe that His fire is working in places you cannot see, undoing what years of struggle could not change.

Practical Steps:

1. Identify one area of bondage you want to see broken and bring it repeatedly before God today.

2. Anoint your head or hands with oil if you can, and declare Isaiah 10:27 over yourself.

3. Spend extra time in worship, inviting the Holy Spirit to saturate you with His presence.

_____

_____

_____

_____

_____

_____

_____

Prayer Points:

1. Lord, let Your anointing destroy every yoke in my life.

2. Break the power of addiction, fear, and oppression over me.

3. Heal every place in my soul that has been damaged by prolonged bondage.

4. Fill me with the Holy Spirit and power for holy living.

5. Let my freedom become a testimony that points others to Jesus.

_____

_____

_____

_____

_____

_____

DAY 13: Taking Authority Over the Night

Key Scripture:

"I will both lie down in peace and sleep, for You alone, O Lord, make me dwell in safety." Psalm 4:8

Supporting Scriptures:

Luke 10:19 | Isaiah 26:3

Not everyone experiences spiritual attacks in the night, yet every believer is called to guard the atmosphere of their home. Some people may feel pressure, unrest, or troubling dreams. Others simply notice their mind becomes more vulnerable when the day is quiet. Whatever your experience has been, tonight is about taking your rightful place in Christ and establishing His peace over your rest.

The night is not something to fear. It belongs to the Lord. Use this time to invite the Holy Spirit to fill your room and your thoughts. Speak the Word of God over your sleep. Declare that your home is covered by the blood of Jesus and that every plan of the enemy is canceled. Ask the Lord to strengthen your spirit as you rest and to renew your mind for the next day.

As you do this consistently, you will notice a shift. Peace becomes the dominant atmosphere. God's presence settles in. Your rest becomes restorative, and your spirit wakes up stronger. Tonight, take authority and dedicate your sleep to the Lord.

Practical Steps:

1. Before bed, read Psalm 91 out loud and pray it over your life and home.

2. Declare God's Word over your rest. Speak Scriptures of peace and protection out loud to set the spiritual atmosphere.

3. Renounce anything that is not from God. Reject fear, anxiety, or heaviness and command every ungodly influence to leave your home.

_____

_____

_____

_____

_____

_____

_____

Prayer Points:

1. Lord, break the power of fear over my mind and emotions.

2. Sanctify my nights and turn them into times of peace and encounter.

3. Cancel every evil arrow and agenda planned against me.

4. Holy Spirit, renew my mind and strengthen my spirit as I rest.

5. Let my sleep be filled with Your presence and prophetic dreams.

_____

_____

_____

_____

_____

_____

DAY 14: Fight for Your Family

Key Scripture:

"For I will contend with him who contends with you, and I will save your children." Isaiah 49:25

Supporting Scriptures:

Acts 16:31 | Psalm 112:2

Fasting sharpens your intercession. It is not only about your own breakthrough. It is about standing in the gap for those connected to you. The enemy fights families because he knows that when a bloodline is redeemed, entire generations shift. Your fast is a weapon God can use to write a new story over your household.

You may see patterns of addiction, poverty, division, or premature death in your family. Do not just observe them. Confront them in prayer. The blood of Jesus speaks better things than every curse and covenant. As you fast, you are contending for brothers, sisters, parents, children, and even those not yet born.

Today, let your hunger become intercession. Call your family members by name before God. Declare that as for you and your house, you will serve the Lord. Heaven hears these prayers. The God who saved the jailer and his household is still visiting families today.

Practical Steps:

1. Make a list of close family members and write one specific prayer next to each name.

2. Pray Isaiah 49:25 over your household, declaring salvation, deliverance, and restoration.

3. Refuse to curse your family with your words. Speak blessing and destiny over them.

_____

_____

_____

_____

_____

_____

_____

Prayer Points:

1. Lord, contend with every spirit contending with my family.

2. Break generational curses and release generational blessings.

3. Save my family members and draw their hearts to Jesus.

4. Heal divisions, unforgiveness, and long-standing conflicts.

5. Let my home become an altar of Your presence and peace.

_____

_____

_____

_____

_____

_____

_____

WEEK 3: ACCELERATION IN YOUR ASSIGNMENT

(Days 15 to 21)

The third week is about stepping into restoration, acceleration, and assignment. After dealing with the heart and confronting the battle, God now begins to build. He speaks of restored years, divine speed, open doors, and provision that carries a kingdom assignment. This is where your story starts to sound different.

In these final days, you will pray into God's timing, His favor, and His purpose for your life. You will see yourself not just as someone who fasted, but as someone commissioned. A watchman. A burning one. A carrier of His presence into your family, workplace, church, and generation.

Week 3 is not simply about finishing a fast. It is about embracing a lifestyle. As the fast concludes, your hunger does not end. Your fire does not go out. You step forward with a clearer sense of who God is, who you are in Him, and what He is calling you to do in the days ahead.

DAY 15: Restoring Wasted Years

Key Scripture:

"Instead of your shame you shall have double honor, and instead of confusion they shall rejoice in their portion. Therefore in their land they shall possess double; everlasting joy shall be theirs." Isaiah 61:7

Supporting Scriptures:

Psalm 126:1–2 | Job 42:10
There is pain that comes from losing money or opportunities, but there is a deeper pain that comes from feeling you lost years. Seasons when nothing seemed to move, where efforts failed, doors closed, and it felt like time passed you by. God does not only restore things. He restores years.

Fasting is an act of faith that says, "Lord, I believe You can redeem what I cannot." You cannot rewind time, but God can redeem it by compressing what should have taken many years into a short season. He can bring you into such grace, favor, and fruitfulness that the story of your life no longer sounds like delay, but like divine surprise.

Today, bring your wasted years to Him. The years of sin, confusion, fear, or stagnation. Do not stay in regret. Surrender them. Ask Him to turn your captivity in a way that will make you feel like you are dreaming. He is the restorer of time and destiny.

Practical Steps:

1. Write down the seasons you feel were wasted and consciously give them to God in prayer.

2. Thank Him that nothing is beyond His power to redeem.

3. Declare over yourself: "My latter days will be greater than my former days."

Prayer Points:

1. Lord, restore the years the enemy stole from my life.

2. Turn my captivity in a way that glorifies You.

3. Heal my heart from regret and disappointment.

4. Make me more fruitful in the coming years than ever before.

5. Let my story become a testimony of redeemed time.

_____

_____

_____

_____

_____

_____

_____

DAY 16: Supernatural Speed

Key Scripture:

"'Behold, the days are coming,' says the Lord, 'when the plowman shall overtake the reaper…'" Amos 9:13

Supporting Scriptures:

Genesis 41:14 | Isaiah 60:22

There are seasons when God moves slowly to build character. There are also seasons when He accelerates His work. Divine speed is not hype. It is when God does in months what others could not do in years, without compromising your foundation. Fasting often precedes such seasons of acceleration.

Joseph went from the prison to the palace in a single day. That one moment did not erase his process, but it did reveal the power of God to change a story quickly. When you fast, you are asking God to bring you into alignment with His timing, not your impatience. Once aligned, He can move you faster than natural processes would allow.

Today, ask for divine speed, but also for divine order. You do not want a promotion that your character cannot sustain. You want speed that comes from grace, not shortcuts. As you seek Him, He will strengthen your feet and cause you to walk on high places.

Practical Steps:

1. Surrender your timelines to God and ask Him to reorder them according to His will.

2. Declare Amos 9:13 and Habakkuk 3:19 over your life.

3. Ask God where He wants you to focus in this season so you can cooperate with His acceleration.

_____

_____

_____

_____

_____

_____

_____

_____

Prayer Points:

1. Lord, align me with Your timing and cancel every demonic delay.

2. Give me hinds' feet to move with grace and speed in Your will.

3. Accelerate overdue answers, promotions, and breakthroughs.

4. Protect me from impatience and wrong shortcuts.

5. Let my life show the difference between human effort and divine speed.

_____

_____

_____

_____

_____

_____

DAY 17: Walking in Open Doors

Key Scripture:

"See, I have set before you an open door, and no one can shut it." Revelation 3:8

Supporting Scriptures:

Isaiah 22:22 | Proverbs 3:4

Open doors are not accidents. They are the result of God's favor and timing. Fasting sensitizes you to recognize those doors and gives you the humility to walk through them well. When God opens a door, no man, system, or demon can close it. Your responsibility is to be ready and obedient.

Many have faced long seasons of closed doors: unanswered applications, delayed promotions, shrinking opportunities. Yet in one moment of favor, God can bring your name into rooms you have never entered, position your file on the top of a stack, and cause people to remember you without explanation. This is not manipulation. It is mercy.

Today, ask God to arise and have mercy on you. Invite His favor to rest on your work, your relationships, and your calling. Favor does not make you arrogant. It makes you grateful. As He opens doors, remember that they are for His glory, not your ego.

Practical Steps:

1. Present your current opportunities and desires before God and ask Him to clearly open and close doors.

2. Pray Psalm 102:13 over your life, declaring that your set time of favor has come.

3. Commit in advance to obey God if He nudges you toward a new opportunity.

_____

_____

_____

_____

_____

_____

_____

_____

Prayer Points:

1. Lord, set before me open doors that no one can shut.

2. Close every door that is not from You, even if I want it.

3. Let Your favor rest on my life, my work, and my relationships.

4. Mention my name to those who need to remember me for good.

5. Use every open door to advance Your kingdom through me.

_____

_____

_____

_____

_____

_____

_____

DAY 18: Prosperity with Purpose

Key Scripture:

"But you shall remember the Lord your God, for it is He who gives you power to get wealth, that He may establish His covenant."
Deuteronomy 8:18

Supporting Scriptures:

Haggai 2:8 | 2 Corinthians 9:8

Finances are spiritual. Poverty is not humility, and wealth is not automatically carnality. What matters is Lordship. Fasting helps break the spirit of lack and selfish striving by re-centering your heart on God as Provider. He gives the power to get wealth, not just for comfort, but to establish His covenant and advance His purposes.

Many are under financial warfare: constant lack, sudden losses, unexplained devourers.

Through fasting and prayer, you can confront these patterns and invite God into your economy. When He blesses, He adds no sorrow with it. His goal is not for money to own you, but for resources to flow through you.

Today, bring your finances to the altar. Repent of any fear, greed, or mistrust in this area. Ask God for wisdom, favor, and ideas. Ask Him to trust you with provision that has an assignment attached, so that you become a channel and not a reservoir.

Practical Steps:

1. Lay out your financial situation before God in honesty and invite Him to take control.

2. Ask the Lord for one practical step of obedience related to giving, saving, or stewarding better.

3. Declare Deuteronomy 8:18 over your life and break agreement with a mindset of lack.

_____

_____

_____

_____

_____

_____

_____

_____

Prayer Points:

1. Lord, break every spirit of lack, debt, and financial captivity.

2. Give me power, wisdom, and ideas to create and steward wealth.

3. Let my finances be aligned with Your kingdom purposes.

4. Raise divine helpers, partners, and opportunities in this area.

5. Make me a generous channel of blessing to others.

DAY 19: Standing in the Gap

Key Scripture:

"I urge you, first of all, to pray for all people. Ask God to help them; intercede on their behalf, and give thanks for them." 1 Timothy 2:1

Supporting Scriptures:

Colossians 1:9 | 2 Thessalonians 1:11

By now, you may feel a shift in your prayer life. You may feel that your prayers are now less centered on yourself and more drawn toward others. This is the work of the Holy Spirit. He is training you as an intercessor, someone who stands in the gap between people and the purposes of God.

Intercessors carry others before the throne when they cannot carry themselves. They push back darkness through prayer. They contend for destinies, families, churches, and nations.

They sense burdens that do not belong to them, yet they pray until God moves. Your hunger, your tears, and your obedience in this fast have prepared you for this. You are not just praying, but partnering with heaven.

Today, embrace that calling. Even if you never preach a sermon, heaven will recognize your intercession. Show God that He can trust you with names, faces, and burdens to pray through. As you continue beyond this fast, He will give you assignments in prayer and victories to steward. This is not a weight but a privilege. To stand in the gap is to stand with God.

Practical Steps:

1. Ask God if there is a specific time of day or night He is calling you to watch in prayer.

2. Choose one area beyond yourself (church, city, nation) and intercede for it today.

3. Write down any burdens or impressions you sense while praying and keep them before God.

_____

_____

_____

_____

_____

_____

_____

Prayer Points:

1. Lord, train my hands for war and my heart for intercession.

2. Make me faithful as a watchman for my family, church, and generation.

3. Sharpen my discernment to know what to pray and when.

4. Let my prayers carry weight and produce lasting fruit.

5. Keep the fire on my altar burning even after this fast.

DAY 20: Keep the Fire Burning

Key Scripture:

"Not lagging in diligence, fervent in spirit, serving the Lord." Romans 12:11

Supporting Scriptures:

Jeremiah 20:9 | Matthew 5:14-16

God never intended for your spiritual life to be occasional sparks followed by long seasons of ashes. His desire is that you live as a burning one, a steady, consistent flame for His glory. Fasting has been His way of clearing the altar, adding fuel, and igniting what He placed inside you from the beginning.

Jeremiah said God's word was like fire shut up in his bones. That same fire is meant to burn in you. Not just when you are in a service, but in your daily routine: at work, in your home, in your conversations. A burning life is one where Jesus is not a compartment but the center. Your decisions, values, and desires all flow from that flame.

Today, present yourself to God again. Tell Him you do not want a temporary fast experience. You want a lifestyle change. Ask Him to keep you fervent in spirit long after this 21 days ends. You are called to be light in dark places, a living testimony that Jesus is real.

Practical Steps:

1. Write a simple personal "yes" statement to God about how you want to live after this fast.

2. Identify one habit you will maintain after the fast that will keep your flame burning.

3. Ask God to show you one person you can encourage or pray for today.

_____

_____

_____

_____

_____

_____

_____

_____

Prayer Points:

1. Lord, I present myself as a living sacrifice. Keep me burning for You.

2. Deliver me from spiritual laziness and complacency.

3. Let Your word burn in my heart like fire that I cannot ignore.

4. Make my daily life a light that points others to Jesus.

5. Seal in me every good work You have started during this fast.

_____

_____

_____

_____

_____

_____

DAY 21: You Shall Reap in Joy

Key Scripture:

"Those who sow in tears shall reap in joy." Psalm 126:5

Supporting Scriptures:

Psalm 30:5 | Philippians 1:6

You have reached day 21, but in the Spirit, this is not an ending. It is a beginning. Seeds have been sown in hunger, obedience, repentance, and faith. Some answers you have already begun to see. Others are still beneath the surface. Do not be discouraged. Harvest always follows sowing.

God is faithful to complete what He starts. The fast may conclude, but His work in you continues. Your tears, your late-night prayers, your early morning declarations, none of it was wasted. Heaven has recorded every moment.

Your testimony is already in motion, even if you cannot see it fully yet.

Today is a day of thanksgiving and sealing. Open your mouth and thank God specifically for what He has done: in your heart, your habits, your hunger, your family, your faith. Declare that this will not be a temporary spiritual high. The fire will not go out. Joy will be your new atmosphere. And as God answers, remember to testify. Your story will strengthen others.

Practical Steps:

1. Write down at least five changes you have noticed in yourself during this fast.

2. Thank God out loud for each one and ask Him to make them permanent.

3. Decide how you will continue in prayer, Word, and maybe regular shorter fasts after today.

_____

_____

_____

_____

_____

_____

_____

_____

Prayer Points:

1. Lord, thank You for everything You have done in these 21 days.

2. Seal every breakthrough, inner change, and answered prayer by Your Spirit.

3. Let joy become my new default, regardless of circumstances.

4. Give me grace to continue seeking You beyond this fast.

5. Use my testimonies to bring freedom, faith, and fire to others.

_____

_____

_____

_____

_____

_____

AFTER THE FAST, KEEPING THE FIRE BURNING

You have come to the end of these 21 days, but you have not come to the end of what God wants to do in you. Fasting was the doorway, not the destination. Seeds were planted in your heart through hunger, prayer, repentance, and obedience. Some fruit you can already see. Much more is still growing beneath the surface.

The greatest way to honor this fast is not only to remember it, but to live differently because of it. Guard the hunger God awakened in you. Protect the tenderness of your heart. Keep short accounts with God. Stay quick to repent and quick to obey. Hold on to the disciplines you started here, even if in smaller ways. Regular time in the Word, worship, prayer, and even occasional shorter fasts will help keep the flame strong.

You may not feel dramatic every day, but do not be moved by feelings. God has worked deeply in places you cannot fully see yet. Trust Him to complete what He began. Expect testimonies in the weeks and months to come. Expect doors to open, patterns to break, and answers to manifest.

Remember, this was never about perfection. It was about pursuit. And you chose to pursue Him. My prayer is that you will walk out of this fast with a steady fire in your heart, a clearer sense of assignment, and a quiet confidence that God is with you.

The best is not behind you. In Jesus, the best is always ahead.

You will confront distraction, hidden sin, evil altars, fear, and generational cycles, not in your own strength, but in the power of the cross.

By the end of this journey, you won't just have completed a fast. You'll have cultivated a lifestyle of hunger, holiness, and intercession that continues long after Day 21.

THANK YOU FOR READING

We hope this book was a blessing to you. To help you dive deeper, we also offer a study guide and e-course videos to accompany it. These resources are great for weekly small-group discussions!

We also offer reading plans on the YouVersion Bible App to enhance your study and integrate God's Word into your daily life.

If this book was a blessing to you, would you also consider leaving a review on Amazon or Goodreads and sharing it on your social media? This will go a long way in helping others discover this book and grow in their walk with God.

For more information and access to all our resources, please visit pastorvlad.org.

PARTNER WITH US

Vladimir Savchuk Ministries offers a number of biblical resources such as courses, videos, reading plans, and books that have been translated into more than a dozen languages, all free of charge. We are also involved in humanitarian aid around the world, helping those in need.

Our desire is that people from every nation would be able to learn about Jesus Christ and grow in their walk with God. Would you consider offering a one-time gift or becoming a partner to help us continue providing these free resources to people around the globe?

We believe that everyone should have access to free biblical content, and your donations and support help make it possible.

To learn more about our ministry's vision and impact, or to donate, please visit www.pastorvlad.org/donate.

OTHER BOOKS

Break Free

How to Get Free and Stay Free

Single, Ready to Mingle

God's Principles for Relating, Dating, and Mating

Fight Back

Moving from Deliverance to Dominion

Fast Forward

Accelerate Your Spiritual Life Through Fasting

Host the Holy Ghost

Build Fire

How to Overcome Storms, Setbacks, and Spiritual Attacks

Make the Devil Homeless

A Biblical Guide to Deliverance from Demons

Available everywhere books are sold in paperback, electronic, audio version.

You can also download a free PDF on www.pastorvlad.org/books

STAY CONNECTED

www.pastorvlad.org

www.vladschool.com

www.facebook.com/vladhungrygen

www.instagram.com/vladhungrygen

www.youtube.com/vladimirsavchuk

If you have a testimony from reading this book, let us know:

www.pastorvlad.org/testimony

If you wish to post about this e-book on your social media, please use tag @vladhungrygen and use #pastorvlad hashtag.